# The PrEssence Method

No, it's not another meditation guide!

Iris B. Willinger

**The PrEssence Method**

*By* Iris B. Willinger

First Edition - Indigo Warrior Press - UK 2022

COPYRIGHT
© Iris B. Willinger - 2022 All Rights Reserved

All materials, including name, logo, method, content, and any other collateral under 'The PrEssence Method' are protected by law. Any unauthorised usage of either the 'name' or materials, (digitally or physically), broadcasting, public usage, copying or re-recording will constitute an infringement of copyright and result in legal proceedings.

And now the 'legal' bit:

The publisher and author are providing this book and its contents on an "as is" basis and make no representations or warranties of any kind with respect to this book or its contents.

The publisher and author disclaim all such representations and warranties, including but not limited to, warranties of healthcare for a particular purpose. In addition, the publisher and the author assume no responsibility for omissions, or any other inconsistencies herein.

The content of this book is for informational purposes only, and is not intended to diagnose, treat, cure, or prevent any condition or disease. You understand that this book is not intended as a substitute for consultation with a licensed practitioner. Please consult with your own healthcare specialist regarding the suggestions and recommendations made in this book. The use of this book implies your acceptance of this disclaimer.

The publisher and author make no guarantees concerning the level of success you may experience by following the advice and strategies contained in this book, and you accept the risk that results will differ for each individual.

"The PrEssence Method" is registered under UK & global copyright law and registered under: Reg. no. 284743801 - Any misuse or other infringement will result in legal consequences (UK court of law).

Book content: Any unauthorised broadcasting, public performance, copying or re-recording, digital distribution or other plagiarism will constitute an infringement of copyright.

# Acknowledgements

*My endless gratitude to all the inspirational people - authors, speakers, friends and strangers on trains I was lucky to encounter and learn from.*

*Thanks to my inner trusted circle of lovely people who always want the best for me, and were there to help with motivation, advice and a loving heart. This goes out to you: Zel, Barbara, Scott and James.*

*And a big THANK YOU to my amazing editor - Joyce Challis - for her dedication, diligent work, constructive feedback and doing a fantastic job on this, and my other books soon to come.*

# About the Author

The development of this 'method' is rooted in my very personal journey of self-discovery and healing, which took me half a lifetime to complete, and that I have now condensed into this little book.

I was born in Austria, alas, I left at 26 to live & work in the US, and later Ireland and France, before making the UK my home in 2001. I had a global career as a senior business consultant, marketing hot-shot and strategist. However, it was never really something that resonated with my heart and soul. Just because I was good at it, I stuck it out a lot longer than I intended.

My true interests culminated much more at the intersection of science and the mystical. I don't regret my career, as I worked with many leaders of multinational companies for 20 years, learnt a lot, and saw the world. Yet, my career also made me realise just how unbalanced and 'half-asleep' and on autopilot most people walk through life.

My consulting roles often became more like counselling sessions even back then. And I am now an accredited

Counsellor & Mindfulness Practitioner and also an advocate for Men's Mental Health, actively helping to end the stigma and silence, and get LOUD about men's struggles!

So, last year, I started creating some self-help books, tools & products, and set-up a dedicated Men's Mental Health project called *Indigo Warrior Soul*. A podcast followed, and there is more to come. You can check it out on Instagram > @indigowarriorsoul

That kind of work ties in well with this book too, as all healing can only be tackled from the present moment.

The development of **The PrEssence Method** was very much motivated by what worked for me. After recovering from childhood & accident traumas, which left me battling anxiety, depression, and CPTSD throughout most of my life, I became aware of the super-power that the present moment holds - and it changed my life.

I took my healing into my own hands, and by becoming fully present, evolved bit by bit, until my days were pretty much entirely lived in that state of presence. 'NOW' became my normal. This 'PrEssence' method - the essence of presence - is my intuitive tool for more personal freedom and it enabled me to evolve faster - especially from the wounds I still carried from childhood. With this book I want to share my learnings in the hope they will inspire you on your own path.

*PS: My own journey of self-development also led me to*

study myself a motley crew of topics, such as: Neuroscience, Spirituality, Quantum Physics, Epigenetics, Psychology, Gnosticism, Shamanism, and many ancient teachings. An eclectic mix, but they are somehow all connected. My enthusiasm for knowledge, love for humankind in general, and rather intrepid spirit have led me to an incredible place... a place of childlike enthusiasm for life with an immense sense of inner peace.

*Follow me on instagram*
*@indigowarriorsoul*

# Introduction

These are strange times we find ourselves in; times of great uncertainty and crisis left, right and centre. A constant global fear-mongering, panic inducing & mass-hysteria aplenty crept into our lives as the 'new normal'. Hence, being able to retain some form of daily equilibrium and to regain more inner peace and resilience are essential. This book can help with that.

The guidance and learnings, ideas, and suggestions compiled here are hard earned, believe me, and I hope they will resonate.

There are many books out there on this thing called 'Now' - but I haven't found a single one that covers it the way I came to it. One of the most inspirational books you may know - *The Power of Now*, by Eckhart Tolle. It was on my

## Introduction

own bookshelf for 20+ years and helped me greatly. You may also have heard of *'Flow-state'* - and this represents part of the concept here. But I seem to have outgrown them and evolved into my own 'method' - that is the baseline of my personal wellness these days.

We all need to start at the very beginning, and that is becoming deeply self-aware of who we truly are, what our minds are about and what triggers us, to get to grips with what being present truly means.

> **"In order to RETAIN more Presence,**
> **and REGAIN more equilibrium,**
> **you need to RETRAIN your mind."**
> Iris B. Willinger

## Prologue

Just to clarify one thing before we get started. On the book cover, where it says: "No, this is not another mediation guide..." - I mean this exactly as stated, and not to criticise meditation. I am all for it! Only, this is not one such book... actually it is the opposite! An ACTION guide of sorts to the Now!

What I wanted to showcase here is, that there are more ways to tap into the 'Presence' than just meditation. After years of research and my own journey of transformation. I simply want to offer a different approach that may work better for you, so you can harness the Essence of Presence in your day-to-day life more actively!

# Chapter 1

> **"NOW is not a place or time,
> but a frequency!"**
> Iris B. Willinger

Being in the present moment is a powerful alignment. If you have ever felt it, you know what I mean. With it, we can more deliberately create and influence the next moment and the next, and the next … to actively create a better future.

For me, it all started 20+ years ago, when I literally 'woke up' and started to unravel the toxic mess of my past. I realised I had lived most of my days in fear or sadness. Fear of the future and sadness over the past, rarely living in the moment or enjoying the NOW - rather fleeing from it, as the awareness of my reality was too overpowering and painful to sit with. I felt unhinged somehow; no belonging, no centre.

It was a revelation when I finally mustered the courage to see my life for what it was. I somehow found the motivation to look closer at how my mind had shaped my (then) negative outlook, and how that had perpetuated (however unconsciously) a very unhealthy set-point and literally sabotaged my life.

It could be described as the biggest self-delusion act I ever pulled off, and it was painful to realise I had spent most of my life mainly surviving, but never thriving.

When it all came tumbling down, it was like waking up from a nightmare, remembering every detail. The clarity was the most painful thing to acknowledge and it came in big waves. But this clarity allowed me to soon make quantum leaps.

The more I dared to deep-dive into my presence, the more I found out about why things had happened as they did and ... why I had become the person I was; what actually triggered me and how I could learn to manage it better. It was a hard lesson, and involved lots of humble-pie eating,

Yet, when I started facing my truth something else began to appear: an inner voice, a kind guidance that supported me all the way. No matter how difficult it got, it kept me going.

> *"I did not realise in the beginning, what a potent and transformational tool I had accessed, and how it would change my life ... for the better."*

Countless ancient books already make a big deal about being present and to 'see the truth in each breath'. Many advocate meditation and self-reflection. There is nothing wrong with that, but this never fully worked for me. What did work however, was a perhaps unusual combination of physical, active, sensual elements, and learning how to manage my breath, and my thinking to steer my emotional experiences better.

But as with all new experiences, the Ego can throw a spanner in the works. So, to tackle the mind and all those obstacles and limiting beliefs ... we need to get 'down n'dirty' with our Ego. It will throw tantrums, behave like a drama queen do stupid, silly, downright dangerous things ... all to avoid changing the status quo.

For the Ego will do everything to keep running the show... until you become aware of 'it' ... consciously. (Book II of the series will deep-dive just into that, and how to overcome Ego traps.)

Strange as it may seem, over the years, even quantum physics and advances in neuroscience have both equally played their part in finalising this book. So please keep an open mind whilst reading on, and enjoy the unfolding of it all ...

# Chapter 2
Being present is making the NOW conscious

**Benefits that being present can provide, if practiced with some consistency ...**

- Decreasing levels of daily stressors
- Having more alertness and focus
- Feeling more alive and whole
- Getting to know yourself better
- Becoming more intuitive
- Being aware of better choices
- Halting and transforming triggers
- Feeling more empowered
- Being able to enjoy moments more deeply
- Becoming more mindful all-round
- Managing your low moments much better

## BEYOND THE CHAOS OF TIME IS ONLY THIS MOMENT

Once in a while, I look back and wonder: How did I ever get this far? The chaos of constantly thinking in either past or future-scenarios is an incredible burden on your system. But, as I realised for myself, it was of my own making, and I felt I had to be its slave; perpetuated by outside demands constantly pulling me away from living in the present. I am sure most of you can relate. My mind was always in hyper mode: pre-judging, worrying, overthinking, reliving. This is not only exhausting, but it is also highly counter-productive to one's (mental) health and quality of life.

Being present, being HERE, NOW …. what does that actually mean to you? Take a deep breath - as deep breathing brings you in touch with you - and allow yourself to reflect on this for a moment. Take your time …

What comes up when you think about being in the moment?

Do you feel anxiety bubbling up?
Is it stressful for you to consider it?
Do you feel guilty?
Is there boredom attached?
Do you try to play it off as unimportant?

Whatever emotions the association of your NOW conjures for you, don't judge them, and simply observe where your mind goes. Detached observation of 'self' is one super-tool. Another potent question to ask yourself is:

*When was the last time you truly felt present in the moment?*

Kids are great at embodying the essence of presence, as it still comes naturally to them to be completely immersed in the moment, to lose track of time; totally carefree and non-attached to any outcome. This is also the place where transformation and fast learning happens easily.

For adults, time seems to move faster and faster: things must be done, stuff to sort, jobs to finish, tasks to complete, places to be, people to see... work, work, work! Responsibilities ad nauseam, and little to no time to just "Be".

I have friends who are even stressed out over 'having' to attend their weekly yoga classes or meditation sessions! Some would benefit to skip a class or two and just walk in nature and marvel. Taking time to anchor yourself in the NOW also means to overcome one thing and cultivate another. I am talking about ...

**Guilt versus Self-Love!**

Unless you set time aside deliberately, this 'Now' I am speaking of will pass you by your whole life - and that would be a real shame. For some lucky individuals, however, being in the present moment is kind of their natural state, they are in the flow of things. You often notice these people, as they always seem to have a lighter energy, and zestier vibe and ... things also seem to come to them with ease. Here is your clue!

Ease and surrender are two other components of being present. But oh, our minds ... tricky things our minds! Always stirring up trouble and making things harder than they need to be.

# Chapter 3
BRAIN & MIND FACTS

Our brain and mind are peculiar, fascinating, downright magical - yet they are not the same. The brain is the factory, and the mind is the foreman so to speak. Recent scientific discoveries have unearthed that our brains can conceptualise in 11 dimensions. Imagine that! And we are already struggling in this 3D world!

But the brain - no matter how clever - is not creating actual reality; don't let it fool you. The mind creates that ... or rather a perception of reality based on our beliefs, the experiences that shaped us, and all kinds of cultural/societal influences we grew up with. But that's all it is - a perception is a mere hue of the truth. Like 52 Shades of Truth!

We could go into lengthy discussions regarding whether

one reality even exists - but for now, let's stick to the here and now.

Perceptions ... this means that your NOW looks and feels different to mine. Your mind facilitates a unique picture of collated life-experience; a cognitive and sensual smorgasbord unique to you. Everyone has a different imprint and different associations with even the smallest of things: likes, dislikes, words, sounds, smells, colours etc. However unconscious this may be, it forms the baseline of your how you experience life itself.

It is clear that we all live somewhat different 'truths'. But what is your NOW exactly? Is it just your imagination? Is it even real? Does it matter at all?

As long as it feels real to you, that's all that matters. Simple as that. Your perception of your reality is not for anyone else to judge, nor can anyone really see the world as you do. That in itself is mind-blowing if you think about it, as it gives you, me, all of us a unique viewpoint we can choose to explore and share, and in doing so expand our horizons and those of others.

The present moment, however, is not a static place – it's much more of a moving feast. Start to think of the NOW as a frequency you can tap into - like a radio station you fine tune. You will know it, as it feels really different when you are 'in it'.

But back to our brains and minds, as they are the gatekeepers to getting into the NOW. A fascinating write-up in MedicalDaily showcases just how amazing and mind-boggling our brains and minds are.

**Here comes the science bit:**

1. Perceptual reality is entirely generated by our brain. We hear voices and gain meaning from what is in essence waves/energy. We think we can see colours and objects, yet our brain only receives signals of reflected photons. The objects we perceive are a construct of the brain, which is why optical illusions can fool our brain and our mind.

2. We see the world in narrow, disjointed fragments. We think we see the whole world, but we are all only looking through a narrow portal onto a small region of space. You have to move your eyes when you read because most of the page is blurry. We don't see this, because as soon as we become curious about part of the world, our eyes move there to fill in the detail before we see it was missing.

3. Body image is dynamic and flexible. Our brain can be fooled into thinking a rubber arm or a virtual reality hand is actually a part of our body.

4. Our behaviour is mostly automatic. Even though we think we are controlling it. The fact that we can operate a vehicle at 60 mph on the highway while lost in thought shows just how much behaviour the brain can take care of on its own.

5. Neurons are really slow. Our thinking feels fast and yet neurons fire only a few times per second and the brain's beta wave cycles at 14-30 times per second. In comparison, computers cycle at 1 billion operations per second. How can neurons be so slow and yet we are still pretty smart?

6. Consciousness can be subdivided. In split-brain patients, each side of the brain is individually conscious but mostly separate from the other. In hypnosis, post-hypnotic suggestions can direct behaviour without the individual's conscious awareness.

Source: MedicalDaily/www.medicaldaily.com

**Our brain and mind are not set in stone …**

The real transformation tool - that can also be our torture chamber is … our mind. It is our thinking, conclusions, judgements, and beliefs that determine our realities - for better or worse - but this is never an objective world view.

**Scientific facts that will blow your mind:**

- We're not actually seeing 'reality'. Our vision runs 100 milliseconds behind the so-called real world.
- Reality is constructed by your brain, and not actually real.
- The brain alone cannot distinguish between what is real and what is fiction. It can only do that by what

we have come to believe, and that has been formed and determined from our earliest childhood on.
- When we change even just a single habit, we literally rewire our brain and build new synapses.

*"If you are hesitant, or even afraid, to find out how your brain and mind work, you will never be able to befriend the present moment. And that would be a real shame. So, learning how to anchor your mind in the present moment will allow you to see another kind of truth - an expanded, different reality - and with it, a much deeper insight into YOU and life itself."*
Iris B. Willinger

Our mind is subjective until we become truly aware of ourselves. I have come to know that there is such a thing as 'the ultimate truth' out there, but it lies beyond the Ego and the veil of the subconscious. Not many will ever glimpse it and I only have a sliver of a view of it, but I can get closer to it when I bring myself into the present moment. And that's when miracles can happen, literally!

Nevertheless, the process is not that easy, as self-awareness comes at a price. It will peel back everything that is not you first and that can be a daunting ride for a while - yet cathartic - especially if you have lived in a 'delusion of self' or have operated out of a victim-state.

But this peeling back is very necessary, because at the

other end of it lies the holy grail of self-empowerment: true peace of mind and freedom. That's not all! Our wonderful brains & minds - as hugely complex as they seem - are also fuelled by some very primal emotions. That's where your EGO comes in.

We are often slaves to our desires, lust, greed, fears, jealousy, vanity, perfectionism ... and this in turn shapes our mind-set and behaviour. This impacts directly on every single relationship we have and how we show up in the world. That is why self-awareness is such a powerful place to get to. This 'PrEssence' method can do a whole variety of things.

It can give you real grounding to tackle negative emotions and bad habits better, as it helps heighten your awareness and can - if you allow it – take you to the root causes of your negative/limited thinking. It can lead you on an amazing adventure of self-discovery... IF you allow it.

One thing is certain, being present is the only place to be when you wish to attempt to change or transform yourself or your life, whether that is in small ways, or in the form of substantial change.

Chapter 4
# DELIBERATE PrEssence
Module I

MODULE 1 consists of many parts, but you can pin them down to three distinct areas:

**Deliberate | Sensual | Creative**

NOTE:

When I first became more conscious of the present moment and started to deliberately get into it, something strange happened. It was not always a comfortable feeling and it could get weird and downright scary at times. That just showed how out of sync I was with myself. So, if you find yourself struggling in the beginning, I recommend you start a journal and write down all you observe and all that comes up for you. It will be a great companion and guide throughout this journey towards your NOW.

> "True presence can only be achieved
> by completely letting go of past & future.
> It is like an act of surrender."
> Iris B. Willinger

Get deliberate darlings!

If you wish to tap into this powerful thing that is your presence, you need to become more deliberate with your intentions, thoughts and actions. But how to do that?

You start focussing on what you are doing right NOW and 'feel' it. It may be small steps in the beginning ... a few seconds, maybe a minute. But as the slogan goes: Every little helps, so keep at it!

With a bit of practice, you can extend these excursions into your NOW. This could take the form of slowing down to enjoy something a bit longer; looking at a flower, really feeling the sun on your skin, tasting a lovely treat, or taking time to really smell a pleasant scent. *Sensually prolonging* a moment means that you need to deliberately SLOW DOWN first. More deliberate focus can get you into the NOW quicker, for longer.

Furthermore, making deliberate NOW-time is crucial. But you don't need to remove yourself from your environment necessarily. You can literally do it anywhere. It's like zoning out for a bit.

## The PrEssence Method

## NOWING = ALLOWING!
Iris B. Willinger

Once you are ready to get into 'the zone'...

- start to tense all your muscles, then relax them
- take a few deep breaths
- look around you deliberately
- use your senses fully to feel out your environment

If you feel like it, you can even say what you see out loud. Verbalising and word association is also a powerful tool to become more present.

**"I spy, I spy with my little eyes ..."**

Following, some very potent tips and strategies that can help you deep-dive into the NOW more consciously.

We all have one or two senses that are more developed, so it is good to find out which ones are more prominent for you and to utilise these in the process of becoming more present.

It is very likely that if you haven't practiced being present, the first emotions that come up will be quite intense, even silly, or awkward, overpowering or anxiety inducing. THAT's normal, yep!

So... get really comfortable with being uncomfortable for a bit lovely folks - after all, you are venturing outside your comfort-zone, and that's always a bit iffy. But stick with it ... these notions will pass quickly.

Another point worth noting is that when you are getting into the present moment, it may highlight a lot of things that you have suppressed. Just let those surface, observe and examine. They are great pointers of what needs work or could benefit from healing and transforming.

Being present - at least in the beginning - is for most people pretty hard to get into. Be patient with yourself and don't let initial feelings and resistance or anxieties put you off. Persistence is key. Little steps are still progress.

Let me ask you a question before we get really nitty-gritty: How conscious are you of all your senses? It's an important question you may well have never been asked before.

**GET SENSUAL**

Yes, you heard me right! Get sensual - and I don't mean in the sexy-sexy way. Sensuality is a great tool to immerse yourself in the present moment more quickly and for longer. So, let's explore all our senses in more depth. If you are lucky to have them all in-tact, count your blessings!

## Vision Smell Taste Touch Sound

Alas, there is another way to cultivate more presence. The main senses stated above are not the only ones we have. Here is a list of our other senses (excerpt from an article of the World Economic Forum by Alex Grey)

**Equilibrioception** – a sense of balance. This is what keeps us upright, and helps us make our way around without getting hurt.

**Proprioception** – knowing which parts of your body are where without looking. It's how we can type without looking at the keyboard, for instance, or walk around without having to watch our feet.

**Kinaesthesia** – sense of movement.

**Thermoception** – we know whether our environment is too cold or too hot. Being able to sense the temperature around us helps keep us alive and well.

**Nociception** – the ability to feel pain.

**Chronoception** – how we sense the passing of time.

## GET CREATIVE

Evolution and creativity go hand-in-hand since the dawn of time.

An essential part of evolving ourselves and anchor us more in the presence can also be achieve through creativity. Without it, life would be pretty boring. There is a whole chapter on how to tap into the essence of presence via creative outlets. And no, you don't have to be an artist to do so!

(THERE WILL BE A WHOLE BOOKLET SOON ON JUST THAT > CONJURING PRESENCE WITH THE ALCHEMY OF CREATIVITY!)

Chapter 5
# SENSUAL PrEssence

Tuning into the present moment
VISUALLY

We are all 'sensual' beings, and how we experience life at any moment is steered by our senses (or lack thereof) however unconscious that may run off.

Our eyes are miracles! Most of us take our eyesight for granted and never give it a second thought. It takes approx. 70 milliseconds for a perception to be transferred into recognition - that's half the time of a blink.

What is even more impressive, is the way the eye delivers the information so that the brain can interpret it. Our brain can recognise and distinguish visual input by mere silhouettes, shapes, hues. What this means is we do not really 'see' with our eyes, we see with our brain.

The eye is merely the tool to feed the brain the intel so it can make sense of it and interpret it. As with all senses, if someone is, for example, blind, the other senses will be much more developed to make up for the absence. As the saying goes - if you look in someone's eyes long enough, you can glimpse their soul.

Providing you are fortunate to have the sense of sight … what do you see right now? How aware are you of your surroundings visually in this very moment? Of yourself and others, the colours, hues, textures, shapes ? What stands out, and why?

What … do … you … perceive?

**How to utilise this visual sense for more presence:**

- Observe something beautiful or interesting for longer
- Blink consciously a few times - it slows down your brain
- Do some mirror work and just gaze at your reflection
- Look at a detail in nature & explore it in all its intricacies
- Focus on something and ask yourself: WHY do I like this?
- Start a visual hobby, like photography, sketching, painting

## Colours Shapes Hues Shadows Light Textures Darkness Brightness
### and even the absence of something...

With all of this, however, there is still one thing we must not forget. All that we see is not actually 'real' since we only interpret things as we perceive them, and this perception is a fickle friend. It is formed and moulded of many things that can all dilute what's 'real', for everyone's reality is only ever a perception. Bit mind-blowing, if you think about it!

This means that the world I see and the world you see can differ greatly, yet neither of us would be wrong.

But once you settle into your being present, you can glimpse a different truth that lies beyond so-called perception. Immersing yourself fully in the Now is able to lift a veil and allow us to truly 'see' things as they are, if we are ready for it. It is quite miraculous really.

Chapter 6
# SENSUAL PrEssence

Tuning into the present moment via
SCENT

A recent article in ScienceDaily states: Our sense of smell plays a major - sometimes unconscious - role in how we perceive and interact with others. How we select a mate, or decide what we like to eat. And when it comes to handling traumatic experiences, smell can also be a trigger in activating PTSD (Post Traumatic Stress Syndrome).

A powerful sense we have there indeed. Did you know that our nose has around 400 scent receptors that are composed of millions of sensory neurons at the back of our sinuses, giving feedback to our brain?

You may have experienced the phenomenon yourself whereby certain smells can literally transport you back in time and have powerful memories attached to them.

. . .

So it's really a good idea to use your sense of smell to 'sniff out the present moment'. You can get into the NOW more easily when you become aware of what you smell - also try closing your eyes - it helps!

This way you can deepen the smelly experience. Scents are also incredibly powerful triggers for emotions, so be aware that a generally nice scent could trigger something unpleasant. You have heard of the phrases: "I can smell danger!" and "Someone smells fishy!" (referring literally to the emotion of mistrust).

Associating scents and smells with emotions is all part of our sensory toolbox. And just like certain smells can trigger negative memories; other scents can help us heal and improve our day-to-day lives.

What are some of your absolute favourite smells/scents?

**How to get into the NOW with your nose...**

- Sniff out your surroundings (literally, yes)
- Introduce new (pleasant) smells in your daily routine
- Hover over food and enjoy the smell of it ... linger, linger ... aaand linger a bit longer
- Re-familiarise yourself with favourite childhood scents
- Tune into nature and let your nose explore natural smells

Iris B. Willinger

**Sweet Sour Clean Woody
Fresh Flowery Medicinal Rancid
Noxious Manly Green Neutral**

Using scents more deliberately - if you are feeling anxious or stressed for example - can help you quickly get some equilibrium back and re-jig that wobbly brain chemistry.

Chapter 7
## **SENSUAL PrEssence**
Tuning into the present moment via TASTE

The juicy way to get into the NOW is simply, savour every bite on your plate, or every gulp in your cup. And here are a few other ways you can dive deeply into the moment using your sense of taste. First, get clear - VERY clear - about your likes and dislikes and then ... become an explorer of new tastes.

Imagine! Each taste bud on your tongue (and there are between 2000-8000) has 50-100 individual receptors. Let that sink in.

What do you like to taste?

What are you tasting right now?

Do you have any favourite flavours?

Some tips to further develop your taste buds and evolve your senses:

- Chew slowly and deliberately
- Really 'taste' what you are eating and drinking
- Explore a new fruit or new dish you have never tried
- Experience the textures of various different ingredients

**Salty Bitter Bland Frozen Fruity Sweet Meaty Luke-Warm Spicy Cold Hot**

Chapter 8
# SENSUAL PrEssence

Tuning into the present moment with
TOUCH

In a world where we have literally 'lost touch' with ourselves, it is difficult to come back to our innate body-sense and 'feel' ourselves. Even more reason to get into the present moment through tactility.

There are 4 touch stimuli we humans have: heat, cold, pressure and pain. Nerve endings transport these stimuli to our brain where they are processed into meanings, warnings, and feelings - this is very simplified of course.

Tactility is my personal favourite sense, as I am a very 'touchy-feely' person. Even as a kid, I had to touch everything. It was simply how my brain made sense of the world around me. To me, it's also a kind of energy transfer. As an adult, I still love to walk barefoot, as the direct feeling of the ground makes me somehow calmer, more grounded. But enough about me - What about you?

Do you like touching or being touched?
Are you tactile (why/why not)?

If you are depressed or suffer from anxiety, then touch can be one of the most healing antidote to your frail nerves.

**Here is what this could look like:**

- Feel the texture of your skin, favourite sweater, hair
- Explore different touch sensations in your environment
- Let your hand glide through water
- Pet an animal
- Enjoy a massage or give one

**Soft Spiky Warm Cold Uneven Smooth Rough Watery Dry Silky Frosty Sharp Organic Slimy**

Chapter 9
## SENSUAL PrEssence

Tuning into the present moment with
SOUND

Listen ... just listen ...

- Listen to all of the noises around you
- Tune into the sound of your own voice
- Play a song and turn it up full volume
- Stand in nature and just listen
- Pay attention to the voices/intonations of people
- Practice being silent once in a while (and enjoy it!)

**Sounds Noises Voices Silence Words**

As we are mostly on autopilot when it comes to our sensing, making each one conscious can also bring up old memories. For example, smell is a potent sense linked to our past. Just find your own sweet-spot and then explore from there. Become a sense-adventurer!

. . .

Writing down your thoughts and feelings, and documenting this journey of sensual exploration, will later provide you with a great source of reflection and give you an opportunity to anchor yourself better in the present moment.

# Chapter 10

Getting into the NOW via
CREATIVITY

As children, creativity came so easy to us, right?! Many adults, however, struggle to be creative. Yet creativity is a fail-safe way to learn, as it means exploring without judgement or forced outcome. It is enJOYment in motion - the best way to learn really.

- Engage in something tactile & make something
- Play with colours and materials
- Become more 'playful with life itself

**Writing Painting Dancing Playing Singing Crafting Acting Decorating Doodling**

When did you last do something creative?

- Tried out a new hobby

- Got messy with colours
- Played a new game
- Done something creative just for the fun of it

## The brain on creativity

What is happening in the brain during periods of heightened creativity? In a published paper: "Robust Prediction of Individual Creative Ability from Brain Functional Connectivity," Beaty and colleagues (2018) unearth the neurological signature of creativity, using sophisticated approaches to identify the neural network activity, the brain-print as it were, which is associated with divergent thinking. They then use that understanding to distinguish more creative from less creative brain activity.

(Resource: Psychology Today/ Source: Beaty et al., 2018)

> " Your future is literally a fictional story
> you 'think' into being, but you can change that script to create different outcomes."
> Iris B. Willinger

# Chapter 11

Deepening the Awareness of BEING present

The Deep-Dive as I all it!

You can go really deep with your awareness using any of your senses at any given time. Most people have 2 main senses that are more active in how they assess their environment.

Finding out what your primary senses are and challenging yourself to then develop those who are not as dominant can lead to real breakthroughs.

The key ingredient for all of us to get into the present moment is (self)Awareness. You now know that the present moment is a movable feast - remember I mentioned FLOW & FREQUENCY in the beginning; that everything is in constant flux – but still, you have to become more aware to utilise the powers the present moment has on offer.

Awareness and deepening of such will not only make this life much richer and more enjoyable, but it will allow you to become more wholesome. And here is the really good news ...

**You**
**can**
**be**
**present**
**anywhere**
**!**

# Chapter 12

Once you practice Module 1 more often, you will soon see a real difference on how you 'walk through your day'. It will also give you insights into your preferences, of what senses and what creative tools are best suited for YOU to get you into the present moment. You can then start deepening that experience 'ad infinitum' - seriously, there are so many layers of NOW, as you will come to realise. Hence I said in the beginning: Now is a frequency, not a set point in time or place.

In the follow up book to this - because getting to grips with Module 1 will be engaging and daunting enough in the beginning, there is a Module 2 - the tricky one, as it goes to town with personal enemy number one>> your EGO!

. . .

But let me emphasise something again. WHO says that you can only be present in a tranquil, quiet, and peaceful environment? Nobody ... right! That's a myth I'd like to demystify, as it is simply wrong!

You can be fully present even in the most hectic, chaotic cacophony sitting in New Delhi airport during a strike or in a traffic jam in central London ... and still be anchored in YOUR NOW.

Your level of presence depends on the consciousness and focus you give and pour into any given moment.

It's all a matter training your mind. It is possible to hold your equilibrium no matter what is thrown at you. Mastering the mind offers a completely new set of tools for life.

Look at athletes performing in front of thousands of screaming fans, battling against opponents, for example - yet they still keep their cool and many 'zone out'. Your mind can be your ally to overcome any ego-traps ... so use it!

And obviously there is always deep breathing - which is a fascinating thing actually.

**Your brain on deep breathing**

Here are some scientific facts that might interest you regarding deep breathing. In a paper I found, it says ...

. . .

*How Breath-Control Can Change Your Life: A Systematic Review on Psycho-Physiological Correlates of Slow Breathing*

*The main effects of slow breathing techniques cover autonomic and central nervous systems activities as well as the psychological status. Slow breathing techniques promote autonomic changes increasing Heart Rate Variability and Respiratory Sinus Arrhythmia paralleled by Central Nervous System (CNS) activity modifications.*

*EEG studies show an increase in alpha and a decrease in theta power. Anatomically, the only available fMRI study highlights increased activity in cortical and subcortical structures. (Resource)*

**Psychological/behavioural outputs related to the above-mentioned changes are:**

- Increased comfort
- Relaxation
- A feeling of pleasantness
- Vigour and alertness
- Reduced symptoms of anxiety, depression, and anger

It is really simple - deep breathing is not only great for your health but also helps you anchor yourself in the NOW better

- so you can make decisions and choices from a more relaxed, less anxious, and more conscious state. That's a Win-Win right there! But ... yes there is a but I'm afraid. I want to talk about this here as I myself experienced it on and off when trying to connect more to the present moment. Old issues and suppressed emotions that are unresolved are given space to resurface when you hold yourself in the present moment.

Don't be alarmed by this, it is actually a good thing, a healing opportunity, but must be addressed properly. Hence, if you feel it is getting overwhelming, you need to seek help from a professional, as I cannot judge what you may have held back and what needs to come out. This is why I also brought up all the creative aspects and senses, as they too can be great tools to facilitate your healing journey if that is what must be done first.

In our day and age, we are often caught on this infinite treadmill of stress and constant 'doing' and 'over-performing'. It is difficult to break this cycle that can wreak havoc on our mental and physical health.

You know that panicky feeling you get the minute you take some 'me time' or try to relax. And even when you relax, you often get distracted and pulled right back into all the chores that are waiting and thinking about what's coming next.

· · ·

**Familiar feelings that can arise when trying to be more present:**

Anxiety | Guilt | Self-Judgement | Avoidance

I have had them all in some form or shape and - even now - some of them creep up once in a while; only now I know how to dissolve them quickly.

Let's examine why some of these feeling can be emphasised when entering yourself into the NOW, as well as the root causes of why these feelings arise when you are actually trying to do something pleasant and relaxing.

1. ***Anxiety:*** *If you start deep breathing or connecting to the present moment, it can also be a physical challenge - as your body might not be used to slowing down and 'feeling itself' - so your brain jumps into alert mode, and this can make you feel anxious, even speeding up your heart rate because it is so unfamiliar. The way to beat this is to breathe through the tension and tell yourself you are safe and it's ok to feel strange.*
2. ***Guilt:*** *Oh, that's a biggie! Often, we do not allow ourselves to slow down or take me-time, and when we do, all kinds of feelings of guilt wash over us. I recommend you tell the guilt to go and get stuffed and that you deserve to learn and explore this. But if you feel permanently guilty when you take a*

*moment for yourself, it is recommended you get to the root cause and examine why you are not comfortable with making self-care a priority.*

3. **Self-Judgement:** *You might judge yourself for 'being silly' or that you are too old for this stuff or that this won't work on you anyway. Many people with mental health issues also have a very self-defeating inner voice and harsh inner critic that prohibits them from enjoying things, or just trying new things and seeing where they may lead. Suspend your judgement and your expectation of what this 'getting into the moment' should be, look or feel like. This only hinders your progress. You need to approach it from a neutral angle really and let it allow to unfold for you.*

There is a lot to be said about 'letting go' to get into the present moment. It is a kind of surrender. This can also cause issue if you are (like I was) a 'control freak' or not used to letting something unfold without 'forcing' it.

Oh, and by the way, this 'NOW' is not a Unicorn - it's quite real, tangible, and achievable. It's actually the 'realest', truest thing we have at our disposal. This concept took me a while to wrap my head around. So, if the past is no longer real and just a collective perception anyway, and the future is just created and fictional, it begs to say NOW is the only 'real' thing we have... and worth befriending. It exists beyond time.

Taking this further - and I bring Einstein into this and a bit of Quantum Science - time itself does not actually exist. Only the concept we made up with our clocks and calendars; so time itself is a smokescreen. Here, I bring you back to the saying I introduced earlier: "Think of the present moment, the now, as a kind of frequency, not a time or place."

And a frequency carries energy and that means NOW is immensely powerful. Like really, really powerful! Imagine we have this power anytime we choose... and the choice to just stop what we are doing at any given moment - never mind the consequences of course, but the choice is there!

One of the 'side effects' of becoming more present for me was more free-thinking and setting much clearer boundaries; this was something I noticed increase the more I tuned into the present moment. I was also bewildered how little I actually consciously chose to do in my day-to-day. In essence, we are not even conscious half of the time of what we allow to happen or how we act.

Enabling 'PrEssence' also deepens the connection you will have with people around you. A kind of clarity and waking up comes with being in the NOW. Something I truly cherish in my life now. If you practice being present with someone, the benefit is that they will feel more heard and seen too. All great additions - when working on improving your relationships across all areas of your life.

A fantastic part of the NOW and being present is also active 'listening' and being ok with stillness/silence. When you have mastered the first level of 'Nowing' as I call it, you will notice that you can literally carry that stillness and listening with you anywhere you go. It is a humbling and emotional experience, as it also makes you stop and actually listen to yourself and what goes on inside you. My revelation was like becoming acquainted with the girl I once was.

**TIP:** Let whatever emerges come up and navigate and breathe through it as best as you can. There may be lots of tears in the beginning (there sure were for me) and I also felt like the lid of a pressure cooker was suddenly off. All part of the process … and there is help if you need it.

And I can't emphasise enough that you need to allow it. Allow yourself to be in it, in the moment. Hold space for yourself there … just be … allow yourself to let go of distractions... and allow yourself to explore it. To me, making the present moment conscious and then going beyond it, is still one of the greatest adventures I can think of.

# Epilogue

**The PrEssence Method** - Making the Essence of Presence conscious with deliberate actioning and sensing, can be life-changing, if you let it. The process of anchoring yourself more in the Now has soooo many benefits, one of which also includes healing through clarity. It takes mindfulness to a new level of emotional intelligence. *Thank you for being present with me!*

Let HOPE float ... 🩶

*Iris*

* * *

A special Men's Mental Health<br>
Guidance Card Deck + Booklet

The PrEssence Method

**SOON TO COME:** The PrEssence Method - Books II & III

EGOdismantling & The alchemy of CREATivity

# Also by Iris B. Willinger

SOON TO COME ...

**The PrEssence Method Series - Books II & III**

BOOK II > EGOdismantling

BOOK III > The Alchemy of Creativity

Watch the space ...

www.irisbcoaching.com